Original title:
Tangled in Ivy

Copyright © 2025 Creative Arts Management OÜ
All rights reserved.

Author: Maxwell Donovan
ISBN HARDBACK: 978-1-80581-726-0
ISBN PAPERBACK: 978-1-80581-253-1
ISBN EBOOK: 978-1-80581-726-0

Vines Whispers and Beneath

In the garden, vines do giggle,
Winding around each twig and wiggle.
They plot and scheme beneath the sun,
Chasing shadows, always on the run.

With every twist, a secret shared,
Whispered softly, no one's scared.
The bees just buzz, oblivious to,
The leafy gossips, it's quite the view!

Secrets Cloaked in Nature's Gown

The trees don dresses, green and bright,
Hiding gossip, out of sight.
Squirrels dart with acorn plans,
While crickets tap in tiny bands.

Daydreams dance in sunny beams,
As flowers flit with pastel dreams.
What's that rustle? What's that thrill?
Pine cones whisper—oh, what a spill!

Shades of Green Entwined

Mossy hats sit on secret heads,
Kittens play where the fairies tread.
Lizards lounge on lazy rocks,
While nature takes off her playful frocks.

Leaves concoct a zany plot,
With nature's groove, they dance a lot.
Oh, the chuckles in tangled vines,
As the wild plants draft their funny lines!

A Journey through Verdurous Labyrinths

Come step inside the leafy maze,
Where every turn finds new displays.
A frog in shades of emerald hue,
Croaks jokes as if he always knew.

Misplaced paths that lead astray,
With silly signs like 'Go this way!'
A rabbit hops, with twitch of ear,
His laughter echoes, loud and clear!

Serenity Veiled in Leaves

A squirrel wears a leafy hat,
While birds debate on where to chat.
Branches dance like they're in a show,
The sun peeks in with a cheeky glow.

Mushrooms giggle beneath the moss,
Leaving crumbs—what a funny toss!
Nature's laughter fills the air,
Twirling leaves with wild flair.

Into the Heart of Nature's Warm Embrace

Underneath the boughs we roam,
Finding sticks that feel like home.
Bumblebees buzz with a playful sting,
While ants march in their little fling.

A fern wiggles in a silly breeze,
Tickling knees and spinning leaves.
Sunlight squints through leafy spaces,
Creating shadows with funny faces.

Vines Spreading like Silent Echoes

Vines stretch out, they're on a spree,
Climbing high like they own the tree.
Whispers bounce from leaf to leaf,
Creating gossip beyond belief.

Laughter crawls up twisted trunks,
While raccoons play with forgotten punks.
Oh, the tales the branches weave,
Each knot a secret to retrieve.

The Canopy of Secrets Above

A canopy stretches like an old quilt,
Hiding antics that nature has built.
Wise owls chuckle, their hoots a tease,
As frogs hop with a splash and wheeze.

Frisky vines giggle under the sun,
Playing tag, oh what fun!
Nature's playground, swing and sway,
Leaves give a wink; it's a playful day.

The Green Veil of Forgotten Paths

In a garden where laughter grows,
A twist of green in comical prose.
Leaves like hands wave in delight,
While gnomes debate who's wrong or right.

A squirrel dons a leafy crown,
As the daisies dance in silly gown.
Their petals shout a joyous song,
As nature's laughter bounces along.

Rabbits hop in frantic chase,
While bugs wear a whimsical face.
The vines scheme a mischievous plot,
In a world where the serious just can't be caught.

Each twist in the path leads to a jest,
In this realm where folly's a guest.
With every turn, a giggle shared,
In a green world where fun is declared.

Grace of the Climbing Winged

A butterfly flips in a dapper suit,
While blossoms giggle with roots in soot.
They flap around, high in the air,
Chasing the wind with comedic flair.

A bird says to a budding vine,
"Your style's a bit over the line!"
The vine just laughs, "I'm here to stay,
I add a twist to the everyday!"

A ladybug struts with a wink,
Making the dew look like a drink.
With polka dots as her guide,
She glides through chaos, filled with pride.

The air is thick with silly dreams,
As petals burst with glowing beams.
Here, the clumsy and awkward thrive,
In a realm where laughter comes alive.

Interlaced Dreams Beneath the Sky

Two snails debate who's fastest of all,
While clouds drift lazily, looking to stall.
A squirrel drops acorns, misses the mark,
And giggles echo long after dark.

In twisted branches, fairies conspire,
To put on a show that many admire.
With shoes made of petals, they prance and twirl,
As the earth's chuckles unfurl in a whirl.

Each leaf is a secret joke to behold,
While shadows play tricks, both silly and bold.
The stars watch on, with a twinkle and wink,
As the night grows rich with giggles to ink.

In this dreamscape where dreams intertwine,
Life holds a joke on the edge of a line.
Where laughter and thoughts freely collide,
Amidst whims of nature, joy cannot hide.

Emblems of the Hidden Cradle

In tangled beds where flowers speak,
A rogue weed plays hide and seek.
With laughter hidden in the thorns,
The humor blooms as the day adorns.

Mice in hats write sketchy plays,
While dirt-streaked worms steal the gaze.
They fashion jokes from roots below,
Creating chaos in a verdant show.

The daisies cheer for their daring friends,
While bumblebees buzz, neglecting their ends.
With each twist and quirk of leafy delight,
Life erupts in giggles just out of sight.

Curling tendrils bind secrets bright,
In a cradle of green, they bask in light.
Here, within laughter's gentle embrace,
Nature spins stories with a smile on her face.

Bound by Lush Enchantment

In a garden where green fingers play,
I found a vine that led me astray.
With a giggle and wiggle, I dodged a sprout,
Who knew that a leaf could chase me about?

The flowers all chuckled, the trees gave a cheer,
As I danced with the petals, fueled by some beer.
I tripped over roots, it was quite the sight,
In a jungle of laughter, I took to flight!

The Serpent of Verdant Dreams

A snake made of green with a glint in his eye,
Promised me treasures beneath the blue sky.
But instead of gold, I found twigs and a frog,
He laughed at my folly, I named him McClog!

In fields of wild madness, I wriggled around,
While the critters all gathered, their giggles abound.
"This wild chase is grand!" I yelled in pure glee,
As I tumbled and fumbled, what a sight to see!

Lattice of Leafy Passions

There's a web in the garden, it's woven with cheer,
Came a rabbit so fast, thought it was a deer!
With hops and with flops, he darted in glee,
Caught up in the branches, he looked up at me.

The roses all snickered, the daisies did dance,
As we played hide and seek, giving fate a chance.
In a tangle of laughter, we spun 'round and round,
This garden of giggles was quite the playground!

Embrace of the Wild Intertwining

The bushes conspired, they whispered and giggled,
As I leapt through a thicket, my knees they tickled.
A squirrel chimed in, "You're caught in the jest!"
He tossed me a nut, like he knew I was blessed!

With vines that were wriggly and branches that prance,
I twirled in the muck, it was quite a fine dance.
The bumblebees buzzed, joining in with a song,
In this wild escapade, I truly belong!

The Weaving of Earth's Forgotten Tales

In a garden lost to time,
The stories writ in vine.
A snail slips on its path,
Thinking it's a lovely rhyme.

The daisies flirt with bees,
In suits of buzzing stripes.
A dance of clumsy steps,
As if rehearsed by gripes.

The hedgehog wears a coat,
Of moss and leaves so sly.
He winks at puzzled frogs,
And hums a lullaby.

With every twist and turn,
Nature's secrets unfurl.
In every nook and curl,
The jester's laugh will swirl.

Edges and Corners Wrapped in Green

Amidst the leafy chaos,
A squirrel holds a feast.
He hoards every acorn,
Declaring, 'I'm the beast!'

Daisies peek from corners,
As if they've lost the plot.
They giggle at the grass,
In their green little spot.

A crooked fence with charm,
Hides secrets long ago.
The shadows hold their breath,
As whispers start to flow.

With mismatched tools and toys,
The gardener forgot to bring.
Yet laughter fills the air,
Despite the quirks of spring.

In the Midst of Nature's Embrace

Beneath a tangled canopy,
The sun spills golden light.
A curious frog leaps high,
Landing soft on the right.

The wind tells silly tales,
Of frogs in tiny hats.
While daisies spread their petals,
Large as chubby cats.

With chattering of crickets,
And a surprising twist,
A butterfly sneezes loud,
Forgetting it existed.

In this playful expanse,
Where chaos can't be tamed,
Nature's joyful giggle,
In every leaf proclaimed.

Intertwined Destinies in the Orchard

Beneath the apple boughs,
A raccoon finds a snack.
His friends all chase their tails,
As if they've lost the track.

The sunflowers roll their eyes,
At gossiping the breeze.
They sway with every word,
In shades of bright uneasy.

Beneath the tart old trees,
The shadows toss and play.
An owl shrugs in slumber,
As night begins to sway.

With laughter under stars,
And whispers in the night,
The orchard's secret lives,
Are woven with delight.

The Embrace of Wild Growth

In a jungle gym of vines, I trip,
Where every step leads to a slip.
The leaves are laughing, oh what a sight,
A dance with nature, wrong feels so right.

A squirrel looks down with a cheeky grin,
While I'm wrestling roots, oh where to begin?
I swipe at a branch, it swats back at me,
Nature's a joker, can't you see?

Stumbling through green, I reach for the sky,
But a bushy branch says, "Not so fast, my guy!"
With each little twist, I twist and I shout,
Who knew gardening led to so much doubt?

Amidst the foliage, I find my way,
Laughing at vines that want me to stay.
In this leafy maze, I can't help but titter,
Being ensnared has never been fitter.

Severed Connections in the Underbrush

I lost my phone in a patch of grass,
A vine, I swear, it gave me a sass.
"Hey buddy," it said with a leafy shake,
"Look up, look down, make no mistake!"

The groundhog nearby is stifling a giggle,
As I play hide and seek with every wiggle.
"Severed connections," I mutter and grumble,
While the weeds clutch my leg like a playful jumble.

Just when I think I'm about to declare,
A thistle pokes through with a prickly stare.
"Chop-chop," it whispers, "to find your way,
You'll have to dance with the weeds today!"

With hands up high, I start to sway,
The rhythm of vines leads me astray.
Who knew underbrush held such delight?
These severed connections feel quite alright.

Currents of the Forest Floor

The forest floor is a slippery sea,
With roots like rivers, inviting me.
I leap and bounce, a kangaroo's fling,
In nature's circus, I'm king of the spring.

A toad croaks loudly, "What's your next trick?"
As I dodge a branch that's all too slick.
"Don't drown now!" calls a ladybug crew,
They watch and laugh at my clumsy view.

A shuffle here, a giggle there,
I'm lost in this game, without a care.
Each step's a surprise, a comical flop,
As I float with the weeds, I just can't stop.

But oh, what a thrill, this forest ride,
With critters and creepers, I'm filled with pride.
These currents of life carry me fast,
In the wilds of whimsy, I'm meant to last.

Hidden Paths, Shrouded in Green

In the heart of the wild, secrets are spun,
With every twist, I'm having some fun.
Paths intertwine like a game of charades,
In this lively riddle, I'm lost in spades.

Laughter erupts as branches entwine,
A bush tries to share a secret divine.
I duck and I weave through leaf-covered trails,
With whispers of mischief in every gale.

A hedge gives a nod, pretending to know,
While I play peek-a-boo with a tomato grow.
"Why rush?" it chuckles, "Take your sweet time,
In this leafy maze, life's a playful rhyme!"

So I skip through the emerald, giggles abound,
Where the roots tickle toes and jesters surround.
In hidden paths, with laughter so keen,
I find joy in the shades of vibrant green.

Whispers of Growth in the Understory

In shadows thick, a secret spree,
A squirrel stole my sandwich, oh wee!
Around the roots, the giggles move,
While leaves play games, they sway and groove.

A snail's slow race, it's quite the sight,
With laughter bubbling, day turns night.
The mushrooms chuckle, wearing caps,
As flowers dance with cheeky taps.

Echoes of Emerald Connections

The vines have gossip, oh yes they do,
Whispering tales from morning dew.
Bumblebees buzz with tales so grand,
Of nectar quests across the land.

A frog croaks jokes in pond's fine swell,
While fish giggle, sharing a fishy tale.
The daisies join in, winking bright,
With petals fluttering, pure delight.

Threads of Life Interwoven with Love

A spider spins a web of fun,
Decorated with drops, a sparkling run.
The ants parade, their march a thrill,
With tiny trumpets, they sing at will.

The breeze joins in, a playful dance,
As butterflies twirl in daylight's glance.
Each leaf a friend, with stories anew,
In nature's arms, we're all askew.

A Tapestry of Nature's Marvels

The grass tickles toes, a mischievous game,
With gnomes laughing lightly, calling your name.
The old oak whispers secrets of lore,
While chipmunks dart, run, and explore.

A dandelion's wish, a sprightly cheer,
Spreading dreams as the skies grow clear.
In this marvelous mix, we find our way,
With giggles and joy, we brighten the day.

The Nature of Obsessive Ferns

In the garden, ferns did grow,
Twisting, turning, putting on a show.
Whispers of leaves in the breeze,
Ferns gossip secrets with such ease.

They stretch and reach for sunlit rays,
Playing tag in funny ways.
With leafy limbs that wrestle tight,
A green ballet both day and night.

One fern claimed a flower's space,
A leafy dance, a leafy chase.
In a twist, the violet sighed,
'Oh please, just let this bloom abide!'

But ferns just giggled, took a stand,
Wrapped in a leafy, friendly band.
Their verdant fun was all in jest,
In their green world, they looked their best.

Ivy's Echo in the Twilight

In twilight's glow, the ivy laughed,
With tendrils twirling, quite the craft.
It snorted softly at the fence,
And pulled its leaves in cheeky dance.

A squirrel watched with narrowed eyes,
As ivy told its leafy lies.
'Oh come on down,' it seemed to tease,
'Join me, let's sway with the breeze!'

Night danced in with a twinkling grin,
Ivy and stars began the spin.
They tangled tales of grass and night,
Stumbling through funny dreams in flight.

The fence just groaned, 'Here we go again!'
But ivy giggled, 'Let's just pretend!'
In rhymes and riddles, they'd confound,
A twisty tale without a bound.

Grappling with Green Serenity

In a patch where greens collide,
The world's a jester, what a ride!
With creeping vines in curious chats,
They plotted pranks, those leafy brats.

One morning dew said, 'Here's my plan!'
To wrestle the garden gnome, if he can.
But as the sunshine brightened the day,
They just ended up in a leafy fray.

The gnome just chuckled, 'What's the fuss?'
While vines were tangled in mischief plus.
'You silly greens, why even try?'
With a wink, he waved good-bye.

He sipped his tea, quite at ease,
While ferns entwined, attempting to tease.
Nature's spice in the evening glow,
A comedy show of greens in a row.

The Cauldron of Verdant Time

In a cauldron bubbling with green delight,
A mixture of ivy under the moonlight.
With giggles and chuckles, they stir the brew,
A potion of laughter with a twist or two.

One vine hiccupped, 'Add a pinch of fun!'
While leaves danced wildly, every one.
'We'll brew up joy till dawn's first light!'
A leafy party, oh what a sight!

The critters cheered, 'We want in too!'
As whispers of mischief in shadows grew.
With each splash, the giggles got loud,
Even the mushrooms formed a crowd.

And as the stars twinkled bright and clear,
The green concoction filled hearts with cheer.
In this comedic fest, they'd find their rhyme,
A world unwind in the cauldron of time.

The Knot of Woodland Secrets

In a forest full of green,
Squirrels hold a secret scene.
Acorns roll and giggles sound,
As rabbits hop just off the ground.

The owls wink with knowing eyes,
While hedgehogs plot their sly surprise.
Twigs and leaves, a playful game,
Nature's mischief, who's to blame?

The woodpecker drumming loud,
Makes the deer dance, oh so proud.
Frogs wear hats made of moss,
In this place, no one is lost.

So come join the merry crew,
In the woods where laughter grew.
Each whisper tells a shady tale,
Among the leaves, we laugh and sail.

In the Heart of the Thicket

In the thicket where we hide,
A hedgehog wears a spiky pride.
Dancing vines in tangled cheer,
Bring laughter to the woodland sphere.

Caterpillars sing a tune,
While fireflies dance beneath the moon.
Chasing shadows, running wild,
In this forest, we're all a child.

Chipmunks tiptoe, nuts in tow,
Winking wide-eyed, 'What a show!'
Bumblebees buzz with zest and glee,
Turning flowers into comedy.

Oh, the thicket, what a sight,
Every corner holds delight.
Nature's laughter fills the air,
In this place, joys we share.

Veils of Forest Mystery

A curtain of leaves swings and sways,
As playful sprites weave funny plays.
Mice in capes, a daring flight,
Hide-and-seek till fall of night.

Rabbits giggle, tails a-bounce,
Silly shadows all around prounce.
Bats wear hats like party guests,
Join the fun, we're all so blessed!

Mysteries of nature, oh so grand,
A treasure map drawn in the sand.
Follow giggles, find the cheer,
In this green labyrinth, we hold dear.

Veils of leaves, they flap and dance,
In this woodland, life's a chance.
With every rustle, laughter grows,
In the heart, the joy just flows.

Where Shadows Dance with Light

Where shadows play and giggles echo,
A hedgehog jives in a moonlit meadow.
Mushrooms clap their little hands,
As the forest twists in funny strands.

Swaying branches hold a joke,
The wise old owl starts to poke.
With witty quips, he brightens night,
In this woods, we find our light.

Fireflies twinkle, blink and tease,
As the wind whispers through the trees.
Chasing dreams along a brook,
Adventurers in every nook.

So join the dance, step out of sight,
In the woods, the world's just right.
With every turn, a laugh will bloom,
In this place, there's always room.

Embracing the Wild Tapestry

In a garden wild and free,
The plants dance just for me.
They twist and twirl in glee,
Chasing bees up in a spree.

A fern wore a hat quite bold,
While a daisy told stories old.
Laughter swayed with each leaf's fold,
Nature's secrets, a joy to behold.

The weeds pranced round in pairs,
Offering up their wild flares.
They teased the flowers, 'No repairs!'
Amidst the chaos, giggles and stares.

Amidst the mess, I roam wide,
Finding humor as my guide.
With every plant by my side,
We skip along, the wild's my pride.

Whispers of the Green Flora

In the shade where plants all chat,
A cactus wore a comedy hat.
It rolled its eyes, said, 'What of that?'
The lilies giggled, 'Oh, just look at that!'

A willow wept for the bumblebee,
Who tripped on petals, oh woe is he!
'Why can't I hover, floating free?'
The daisies snorted, 'Come join our spree!'

The roses blushed, but not from shame,
As they whispered sweet funny names.
'The tulips are wild, not at all tame!'
They tossed their petals, fanning the flame.

In this lush, leafy cacophony,
Each plant brings humor, oh can't you see?
A comedy show in green harmony,
Laughter blooms beneath every tree.

Nature's Spiraling Adoration

A vine wrapped round the old oak tree,
Said, 'You're my favorite, can't you see?'
With a curl and giggle, fancy-free,
Their love was wild as could ever be.

Meanwhile, the grass rolled with delight,
Telling stories into the night.
While crickets chirped and stars shone bright,
The flowers joined in, a funny sight!

Moss, like a grandpa, grew ever wise,
Sharing tales of tiny fireflies.
'In a world of plants, we wear our ties,
With laughter, not tears, beneath clear skies!'

A budding romance, a leafy cheer,
In nature's arms, there's nothing to fear.
So come join in, we'll persevere,
With every whisper, fun will appear!

Vines of Desire and Delight

The vines did twist and dream all day,
In their leafy dance, they'd sway and play.
'Oh, what a game we're in today!'
They laughed aloud, 'Who's leading the way?'

A polka-dot plant named Max,
Tried pulling off the latest hacks.
It tripped on roots, and then it acts,
Sprouting giggles in mischievous packs.

One flower blared a trumpet note,
While another rode a tiny boat.
Together they laughed, tossing a quote,
'Let joy be our grand antidote!'

So here we frolic, boundless, bright,
In this green wonder, pure delight.
With every twist, it feels just right,
Nature's humor, a joyful flight.

Where Nature's Threads are Woven

In a garden where green vines roam,
They trip you up as you call it home.
A squirrel steals your lunch with glee,
While plants nod, saying, "Look at me!"

The daisies giggle at your plight,
As you wrestle with weeds, what a sight!
The sun peeks through with a cheeky wink,
While you ponder just how to think.

Lizards dance upon tangled trails,
While bees buzz past with silly tales.
As you muddle through this leafy maze,
You can't help but laugh, caught in nature's plays.

So here you are, a jester of green,
With plants as your props in this funny scene.
Nature's threads are woven tight,
And in this mess, the joy feels right.

Bound by the Garden's Secrets

The roses whisper dirt on the daisies,
While you fool around, being a bit crazy.
The herbs plot mischief in the bright sun,
And in this chaos, you think it's fun!

The tomatoes chuckle, bright red and round,
As you stumble and trip on the soft ground.
The carrots peek up, oh so sly,
"You can't catch us!" they seem to cry.

Swirling and twirling, leaves in a spin,
As you chase after that cheeky grin.
With nature's chorus singing your tune,
You dance with the flowers beneath the moon.

Bound by the secrets of green all around,
You're laughing too hard to wear a frown.
In this garden of giggles and jest,
Each leaf a story, a plant's little quest.

Encircled by Life's Green Embrace

In a jungle of green, you look quite bizarre,
With ferns as your friends and a vine as a spar.
The breeze tells jokes through fluttering leaves,
While you chuckle aloud with all that it weaves.

A butterfly lands right on your nose,
You sneeze and it giggles, oh how it goes!
Saplings bow down as you strut by,
With nature as your fan, oh my, oh my!

The weeds play pranks, disguising the ground,
As you hop and skip, feeling quite profound.
The grass tickles feet, oh what a delight,
With nature giggling and keeping it light.

Encircled by life in a quirky embrace,
You tumble and laugh, it's a merry chase.
In the chaos of green, you find your own grace,
As laughter blooms brightly in nature's own space.

A Lattice of Nature's Design

A hedge maze of giggles, a labyrinth of cheer,
You search for the path, but where is it, dear?
The daisies conspire with mischievous grins,
As you fumble your way through this game that it spins.

Vines create puzzles; can you solve this one?
Two pansy-eyed friends have a joke in the sun.
You slip on a leaf and roll down the hill,
The garden erupts in oh-so-sweet thrill.

Rabbits hop by, they know all the tricks,
As you tumble around, caught up in the mix.
With petals as pillows and roots intertwining,
The laughter cascades, and all it feels binding.

A lattice of laughter, sunbeams so bright,
Nature's own puppet in a whimsical flight.
Each twist and turn, more funny than planned,
In this garden of giggles, you take a stand.

Shadows of the Climbing Green

In a garden filled with leafy beer,
The plants conspired, oh so near!
They wrapped around chairs for a sit,
Leaving the guests where they won't fit.

Squirrels played tag in the webbing green,
Chasing shadows, if you know what I mean!
A wild dance of green vines in a whirl,
While I tried to untangle my curl.

They charged at my ankles, swift and spry,
I yelled, 'Help!' as I waved my hand high.
The neighbors chuckled, oh what a sight,
With ivy as my uninvited knight!

So now I laugh in the jungle's embrace,
Dancing along in this leafy race.
I'll claim my throne in this climber's spree,
With nature's giggles all around me!

Clutching Threads of Nature's Heart

Vines peek through windows, a hearty grin,
They wrap around yearbooks, what a win!
Said, 'We're the pages to your leafy dreams,'
But they nearly caught me in their schemes!

A flower burst forth with a laugh so loud,
"Join our parade, come on, be proud!"
I slipped on petals, fell in a heap,
They chuckled and whispered, "Count your sheep!"

With each tug on my pants, I felt a tease,
These rebellious greens brought me to my knees.
They danced around me, I just couldn't flee,
As if they knew I was meant to be free!

Now I'm a jester in this leafy play,
With vines as my crew, come what may.
Oh heart of nature, you've caught me anew,
Your threads spun tight, yet I laugh with you!

Veils of the Vivid Wilderness

The forest wore a gown of bright green lace,
Pretending to hide in a sneaky space.
Each petal a wink, a mischievous jest,
While critters convened for a wild fest!

Bamboozled by blooms, I tripped and rolled,
Getting tangled in nature, oh, how bold!
They grinned as I wobbled like a dippy fool,
Conspiring with ferns, they broke every rule.

"Join us!" they cried with a botanical cheer,
As I gasped for air among branches unclear.
In a labyrinth of laughter, I lost count,
Of the leafy companions that made joy mount.

Through giggles and gaffs, the sun kissed my hair,
Creating a comedy in the vibrant air.
In wild entrapment, I found the fun,
With veils of wilderness—oh, what a run!

Ivy's Caress in the Moonlight

Under the moon, the shadows danced bright,
A leafy embrace stole the cool night.
Brought in as dinner, and now I was prey,
Attempting to shuffle, I was led astray.

The ivy entwined like a warm, fuzzy hug,
Said, "You look comfy, come give us a tug!"
As the moonbeams shimmered on every leaf,
I giggled and squirmed, what a silly thief!

With laughter like whispers, they tangled my hair,
I fought with the foliage, but they'd never care.
A masquerade of mischief revealed under stars,
Fashioned by greens, I became one with their bars.

So here I recline with my leafy friends,
In a soft sprawl where the wild never ends.
Beneath the moonlight, I find my delight,
Sharing my night with the vines of sheer might!

Patterns Born from Wild Overgrowth

In a garden where secrets hide,
Laughter dances, sprightly and wide.
Plants wear shoes of mismatched hues,
In sunny spots where giggles ooze.

A hedgehog dons a leafy hat,
While a snail claims the title of 'splatt.'
The daisies gossip, the trees conspire,
As ladybugs play on a wire.

The roots are plotting a prank so sly,
A flower's wig in the breeze might fly.
With every splash of quirky shade,
A whimsically wild parade is made.

In overgrowth where chaos reigns,
All the critters mimic loud trains.
Chasing shadows, they squeak and squeal,
In this jungle, joy is surreal.

In the Shadow of the Climbing Green

Vines weave tales of frolicsome fun,
With a bright sunbeam that's never done.
They twist and coil like a merry snake,
Playing tricks, causing quite the shake.

A frog in glasses proclaiming he's wise,
Gives fashion tips to a bird that flies.
As mushrooms hold a rowdy dance,
The squirrels watch with a playful glance.

Sunflowers bow with their heads held low,
While ivy whispers, 'Hey, watch me grow!'
Bouncing back from a sunny affair,
The garden's humor is everywhere.

In shadows where comedy sprouts with glee,
Each vine a jester, wild and free.
With rustling leaves that cheerfully tease,
Nature's laughter rustles in the breeze.

Fragments of Life Amongst the Vines

Lost in a maze of emerald threads,
Where wildness hums and curiosity spreads.
A cat wears a crown of blossoms so bright,
Charming the bees in their buzzing flight.

Chasing tails and looking for snacks,
The rabbits dare to make bold tracks.
While whimsical crickets sing their tune,
At twilight beneath the glowing moon.

A swing made of leaves sways oh-so-gay,
Where chipmunks gather for a play day.
Each acorn's a treasure meant to be shared,
In this haven that laughs and is prepared.

Fragments of laughter, snorts, and squeaks,
In a tangled world where no one speaks.
Just hilarious antics that make life bright,
In the garden's heart, joy takes flight.

A Green Shroud of Yesterday's Whispers

Underneath a blanket of green delight,
The past giggles in the soft moonlight.
Memories coiling like strings on a harp,
Playing tunes that make the heart spark.

Old gnomes gossip while peeking around,
In this lush realm, laughter is found.
With roots that wear mismatched socks,
And trees that tickle passing rocks.

A stroll through the chaos yields a grin,
As nature's mischief begins to spin.
Rolling along with a spirited bounce,
Every leaf holds a tale to pounce.

In whispered secrets and whimsical sighs,
The vines reveal their silly ties.
With nature's humor dressed in green,
A shroud of laughter reigns supreme.

Shadows of the Embracing Foliage

In shadows where whispers play,
A squirrel's dance steals the day.
Leaves giggle as they sway wide,
Unruly roots need a guide.

A hedgehog prances with flair,
Bobbing hats of green everywhere.
Puddles mirror laughter's chase,
Every turn, a leafy embrace.

Sunbeams sneak through leafy curls,
As beetles strut, flashing their pearls.
Frogs croon tunes, making a show,
Raindrops applaud the vibrant flow.

In this forest, always unfurled,
Funny antics make the world twirled.
With giggles echoing through the thicket,
Join the revelry, don't you forget!

Life among the Untamed Vines

Grinning greens climb up the wall,
Vines declare, "We're having a ball!"
Lizards lounge with lazy grins,
While buzzing bees buzz wild spins.

Squirrels play peek-a-boo, oh so spry,
Challenging the clouds in the sky.
Bouncy blooms dance a jig,
In garden plots, the fun is big.

Beneath the canopy, shadows flicker,
Giggling worms make the soil quicker.
Butterflies swoosh with vibrant flair,
Tickling petals, a funny affair.

When sunlight breaks with joyous beams,
Nature laughs, igniting dreams.
Join the chorus, let laughter grow,
In untamed vines, the fun will flow!

Flora's Gentle Surrender

Petals flutter, soft and bright,
Whisking worries out of sight.
A bunny hops with curious glee,
Chasing shadows, wild and free.

Dandelions wave with delight,
Whilst ants pull pranks, oh, what a sight!
Flora sighs in gentle waves,
Hopes and giggles, a path it paves.

A bumblebee buzzes with style,
Softly settles, rests for a while.
Silly squirrels play chase and dart,
In this garden, laughter's an art.

Nature's jester, in every hue,
Glances shared in the freshest dew.
Join this frolic of sheer surrender,
Where laughter blooms as a heartfelt tender.

The Resonance of the Wild Headdress

A crown of leaves upon her head,
Dancing to tunes the forest said.
Flowers giggle as breezes tease,
While twirling branches laugh with ease.

A fox winks, plotting some schemes,
Whispers shared in radiant beams.
Grass tickles toes as they prance,
Inviting all to join the dance.

Bouncing blooms, colors so bright,
Join the revelry, day turns to night.
With twinkling stars above the glade,
Nature's laughter won't ever fade.

In every rustling leaf's embrace,
Find a moment, a happy place.
Embrace the joy where wild hearts nest,
In this folly, you'll find the best!

The Stillness among Twisting Vines

In the garden, oh so sly,
A snail zips past, oh my oh my.
Leaves whisper secrets to the ground,
While frogs croak jokes that astound.

A squirrel scampers up a tree,
With acorns stacked as high can be.
"Who has time for all this haste?"
Said a turtle with a leafy taste.

Bugs dance lightly in a band,
To music only they can understand.
Nature giggles, with a wink,
In this chaotic green precinct.

So when you stroll, don't forget,
The funny things that you can get.
Among the curls of ancient vines,
Life's humor cleverly entwines.

Ivy Secrets Under a Moonlit Veil

Under moonlight, shadows play,
With creatures dancing, come what may.
A raccoon flips a trash can lid,
Grinning wide like a cheeky kid.

A wise old owl, with glasses askew,
Mocks the night like he always knew.
"Who needs wisdom in their stride?"
When laughter's hiding side by side?

The night bugs boast of wild romance,
While fireflies blink, inviting chance.
"Catch me if you can," they gleam,
In a waltz of hilarious dreams.

With whispers shared, beneath the light,
The ivy's truth, out of sight.
Silly secrets in the dark,
Echo softly, a merry lark.

Treading Softly in Nature's Grip

With each step, a squish and a slide,
Nature giggles, I can't hide.
Mud and grass, quite the pair,
Who knew that walking's a clownish affair?

A bumblebee buzzes with a cheer,
Inviting me to join its sphere.
"Come and dance, you goofy soul!"
Where dandelions take their stroll.

A feathered friend, all puffed and round,
Sings of mischief all around.
"Why worry, when the sun is bright?
Just laugh and twirl, it feels just right!"

So skip along that winding track,
With laughter echoing, there's no lack.
In nature's hand, we freely slip,
In this joyful, uproarious grip.

The Intricacies of Leafy Threads

Among the leaves, a tangle grows,
With chattering squirrels stealing shows.
A wise old vine sings low and sweet,
    To the rhythm of tiny feet.

A misfit flower, bright and bold,
Tells tales of sunshine, ice, and cold.
"Why fit in, when you can stand out?"
Amidst the greens, laughter's about.

Beneath the leaves, a critter spies,
Filling the night with curious eyes.
"Just what secrets could they keep?
When giggles echo, hiding in sleep?"

So weave through gardens, and don't be shy,
The humor blooms where wild things lie.
Life's wittiness, in nature's threads,
A playful breeze, where laughter spreads.

Ascending the Verdant Labyrinth

In a garden so wild, my hat went astray,
A squirrel now wears it, that rascal, oh hey!
I follow the path, it twists and it turns,
Wishing for GPS, my patience it burns.

Leaves whisper secrets, but none that I know,
With twigs in my hair, I put on a show.
A caterpillar winks, I jolt in surprise,
Is this nature's way to pull pranks in disguise?

I step on a branch, it cracks like a joke,
A frog leaps nearby, but it's me who is choked.
The trail is a riddle, I swear it's a game,
But I'm lost in the green, and I'm not sure who's to blame.

Yet laughter erupts from the foliage deep,
As nature conspired, I stumble and peep.
My adventure is funny, though tangled for sure,
In this maze of green, I giggle and endure.

In the Grasp of Nature's Clutch

Stuck in the bushes, oh where did I stray?
A hedgehog is watching, will he join my ballet?
My shoelace is tangled, with roots in a bind,
Trying to escape, but this place is unkind.

I shout to a bird for some help from above,
He just chirps a tune, no assistance, no love.
A snail glides on by, laughing slow with delight,
'You'll get there someday, just don't miss the night!'

My scarf's now a vine, a fashionable choice,
The leaves join my party, they giggle, rejoice.
A monarch flies past, she raises her brow,
'Fashion week's cancelled—your style's outta wow!'

Yet here in this mess, I dance with the breeze,
Nature's odd humor puts my mind at ease.
Though entangled and tripped with a smile, I agree,
Nature's clutch is a riot, come join the spree!

Entwined by Nature's Grasp

I wandered through vines, thought it'd be delight,
But oh, what a tussle, my jeans are too tight!
Green fingers are tugging, they want me to stay,
In nature's embrace, I'm part of the play.

A squirrel now insists on my shoulder as throne,
He claims I'm his buddy, though I'm not well-known.
We chat about acorns and plans for the day,
While I'm stuck in the ferns, I'm now his bouquet.

Old leaves gossip, the shrubs roll their eyes,
A flower sings loud, oh, what a surprise!
'I've seen better styles than your tangled maze,'
But here I will frolic through nature's fun blaze.

Yet laughter abounds in this foliage fray,
With vines as my mate, I happily sway.
Though gripped by green fingers, I can't help but grin,
This wild, wacky life is where the joy begins!

The Weight of Verdant Shadows

In shadows of green, I think I have weight,
A feathered friend laughs, 'Come share your fate!'
With ferns wrapping round me, I feel quite the queen,
Though ants march in line, not quite what I mean.

I trip on a root that just loves to play,
With every step forward, it pulls me away.
A snake gives a wink, in a glamorous show,
While I dance with the weeds, where else would I go?

Petunias are poking, they call me by name,
They summon more mischief, it's all just a game.
I giggle and whirl, in a circus of green,
A whimsical riot, a nature routine.

Though shadows loom large, there's light in their mix,
With every mishap, I perfect my tricks.
In this green-clad whirl, what a sight to behold,
Life's tangled with laughter, a story retold!

Spirals of Life in the Garden

In the garden, plants do dance,
With ivy's laugh, they take a chance.
A sunflower trips, a rose falls flat,
All while a worm wears a dapper hat.

A gopher fumbles, digging with glee,
While butterflies play hide and seek, oh me!
The daisies gossip, the grass shakes its head,
As a ladybug rolls, 'I'm happy, be fed!'

Bumblebees buzz, doing their jig,
While spiders throw webs, a sticky gig.
The mint jokes about being a breath fresh,
As vines weave tales of rebellion, oh how they mesh!

But amidst this chaos, joy takes flight,
In spiraling petals, a comedic sight.
Who knew a garden could be so spry?
With chuckles of green beneath the sky!

A Maze of Twisting Tendrils

In a maze of greens, I twist and twine,
Chasing garden gnomes, plotting a line.
"Excuse me, sir!" yells a cheeky vine,
"Squeeze in tighter, let's dine on sunshine!"

The carrots giggle, "We're stuck in our hole!
But look at the cabbage, having a roll!"
While tomatoes grumble, stuck in the fray,
With stalwart peppers, they plot and they play.

A squirrel scampers with mischievous glee,
Spreading the chaos for all to see.
Through twirling ferns and winding paths,
Laughter erupts, escaping the wraths.

"Do you see the squash? It's doing a twist!"
In leaps and bounds, it cannot resist.
The garden's a stage, each leaf a star,
Waving and laughing, oh, how bizarre!

Echoes of a Leafy Sanctuary

In the leafy halls, whispers resound,
Of squirrel debates and the worms underground.
The ferns get feisty, as shadows play tricks,
While daisies recite their poetic licks.

"Hey, did you hear?" says the artichoke proud,
"I outgrew my pot, yelled 'let's face the crowd!'"
A broccoli chuckles, puffing out its chest,
"Good luck, my dear, you haven't seen the rest!"

The ivy cascades, with tales so absurd,
Like how caterpillars dreamed of being birds.
In this sanctuary, laughter won't cease,
Even the soil seems to giggle in peace.

Nature's their stage, antics abound,
In echoes of green, joy truly is found.
"Let's dance in the mist, shake our leafy tails!"
In this jovial garden, mirth never fails!

Blossoms in the Midst of Chaos

In the midst of chaos, blooms take a stand,
With petals that wag, just like a band.
"Here I am, daffodil, singing in blue!"
While tulips do pirouettes; oh, what a view!

The bees are buzzing, such curious sights,
As roses throw parties on warm summer nights.
"I'm the Queen!" yells the peony, sweet and round,
While violets whisper confessions profound.

Lively anemones bounce in delight,
While in the corner, a cactus looks bright.
"Watch me, I'm spiky, but don't run away!"
In this floral quarrel, laughter holds sway.

As sunbeams cascade, wrapping kin in light,
Blossoms know chaos is pure comedic might.
In gardens of giggles, growth and surprise,
Beauty blooms wildly; love never dies!

Whispers of the Emerald Veil

In the garden, vines take charge,
They whisper secrets, oh so large.
A squirrel slipped, a twig went snap,
He waved his tail, said, "What a trap!"

Green tendrils tickle at my feet,
I danced with shadows, what a feat!
A hedgehog laughed, rolled up in glee,
"Come join the party, come swing with me!"

Mossy hats on flowers' heads,
They sway and giggle in their beds.
An owl hooted, "Where's my tea?"
"In this mess, look—just follow me!"

With every step, I twist and twirl,
In this green world, I spin and whirl.
The vines conspire, giggles fly,
In a leafy riddle, oh my, oh my!

Entwined in Nature's Grasp

A frog on a leaf, a silly sight,
He croaked a joke in the moonlight.
With vines and roots on his head so grand,
He said, "I'm just the king of this land!"

Beneath the boughs, the shadows clash,
A rabbit tripped on an ivy stash.
"Who put this here?" he asked in jest,
"Next time I'll wear my hopping vest!"

With laughter echoing through the green,
Even the beetles know what I mean.
A prankster bug swings from the vine,
"Join our circus, it'll be divine!"

The air is thick with mirth and zest,
In this leafy maze, we jest and rest.
A dance of color, a gust of cheer,
In nature's grasp, all is clear!

The Green Embrace of Shadows

Underneath the twisting greens,
A caterpillar shares his dreams.
"Just waiting for my turn to fly,"
He grinned and winked, "Well, bye-bye!"

Beneath the leaves, a party brews,
Tiny critters in funny shoes.
"Step right up, take a chance,"
A snail in shades starts an odd dance!

The sun peeked through, a cheeky grin,
And suddenly, all chaos did begin.
A raccoon shouted, "Join the fun!"
With acorns flying, the day was won!

The shadows grew in playful light,
As laughter bubbled through the night.
We spun and we twirled, no hint of rue,
In the green embrace, just me and you!

Secrets Woven in Canopy

A Robin with a crooked hat,
Was sharing tales of this and that.
"Did you hear what the branches said?
It's all a mess but let's not dread!"

The leaves above were having fun,
They winked at the sun, oh what a run!
"Join us now, we've got the beat,
A rhythmic rustle, come feel the heat!"

With whispers dancing on the breeze,
A fox declared, "Oh I'll appease!
I've packed some snacks, just take a peek,
In this leafy realm, we're all unique!"

Secrets spun in emerald threads,
With jests and giggles filling beds.
In the canopy, we'll forever stay,
Where laughter grows and shadows play!

The Silent Symphony of Climbing Flora

A lazy snail spilled juice on me,
In leafy choir, they sing with glee.
Worms with their banter, so quite absurd,
Raucous parties with no one heard.

A fern in frills, just prancing about,
While mushrooms giggle, with no room for doubt.
A buzzing bee debates with a mouse,
Who's the best dancer in this green house?

In shade, the ants throw a grand parade,
With raindrops plopping, a wet charade.
Hedgehogs snigger, they just can't see,
That life's a party, not just a spree.

So raise your larks and stretch your vines,
In this leafy den where joy entwines.
A symphony plays, without a score,
Nature's giggles, who could ask for more?

Underneath the Cloak of Greenery

Under the cloak of leafy drapes,
A squirrel recounts its tales of scrapes.
The vines whisper secrets, quite the tome,
While beetles plot for a cozy home.

A raccoon juggling acorns, quite the feat,
Wearing a mask, but it's still discreet.
In bushes, the chatter of crickets beams,
Life's a comedy with comedic dreams.

In shadows, the path is uncertain and sly,
With each step, many friends stop by.
A rabbit winks, it hops in delight,
Waving to daisies, glowing white.

Beneath this canopy, joy isn't rare,
With twists and turns, everywhere to share.
Under the cloak, the laughter flows,
In every corner, glee just grows.

Embracing the Unruly Wilderness

In the wild of weeds, there's fun to be found,
With critters and giggles, it spins all around.
Thistles throw shade, such playful jest,
A party of chaos, but feeling blessed.

The feral laughter of leaves that sway,
With roots that trip you, what a display!
A hedgehog prances, with poise and flair,
While wildflowers chuckle, without a care.

A thicket of mischief, a tangle of cheer,
Every twist in the trail brings friends near.
Follow the giggles where laughter resides,
In the unruly green, joy abides.

The wilderness winks, it's perfectly fun,
With merry misfits, life just begun.
Embrace the wild, let your spirit roam,
Amongst all the laughter, you'll find your home.

Veins of Life in the Woodland

In the wooded veins, a giggle flows,
Curly vines tickle, a whimsy that grows.
With ants in tuxedos, they march in sync,
Confident creatures, really on the brink.

Mossy carpets boast of their craft,
While fairies share jokes, quite the laugh.
The trees gossip low, whispering cheers,
About all the fun from past few years.

A dance of shadows where sunlight plays,
A snicker from owls, they've seen better days.
With critters beneath and above in thrall,
Each rustle and rustle, a woodland ball.

Every root's a story, a tale to be spun,
In veins of laughter, we all become one.
So grab a twig and dance through the glen,
In the woodland's embrace, let joy begin!

Mossy Memories Enveloped in Green

In the woods, I took a stroll,
Got stuck in a mossy roll.
A squirrel laughed as I fell down,
My hat now wears a leafy crown.

Nature's blanket, soft and sly,
Hiding secrets, oh my my!
Twirling leaves, they danced and spun,
Who knew being lost could be such fun?

A mushroom giggled right by my toe,
"Welcome, friend! You're moving slow!"
I waved to frogs, they croaked a tune,
The trees chuckled, under the moon.

With each step, I found a new game,
Nature's tricks, none were the same.
So here in green, I'm stuck in play,
Making mossy memories today!

Murmurs from the Canopy Surfaces

Beneath the leaves, whispers abound,
A chatty breeze swirls all around.
Branches point and giggle with glee,
As I trip over roots, just to be free.

The canopy smiles, it's all in good fun,
Calling my name like a mischievous pun.
"Hey there, human, you look quite lost!"
I blink and ponder the price of this cost.

Birds chime in with silly remarks,
As I dodge acorns thrown by the larks.
A teacup of rain drips down on my face,
I chuckle and look for a new hiding place.

In this tangled puzzle, I can't help but grin,
Laughter and joy dance where I've been.
Here's to the whispers among the trees,
Every rustle is just nature's tease!

Bound by the Beauty of the Wild

I wandered deep where the wild things play,
Caught in a flower, much to my dismay.
The petals chuckled as I tried to flee,
"Izzy, stay! Come smell the glee!"

Butterflies fluttered, performing a show,
While I laid tangled in grass just below.
The daisies leaned in, gossiping close,
They know my secrets, and I feel morose!

A bumblebee buzz, like a tiny parade,
Demanding my dance, I'm caught in the shade.
With each little step, I lose all my grace,
Yet nature pulls me into its embrace.

But who wouldn't giggle at this sight?
A human in bloom, oh what a delight!
Bound to the beauty I find all around,
In laughter and whimsy, my heart's tightly wound.

The Snare of Nature's Hand

In the backyard, I found a vine,
Wrapped around my leg, quite divine!
"Hey there, friend! Let's have some fun!"
The vine replied, "You've nowhere to run!"

The flowers laughed, bloomers in rows,
They waved at my feet, struck silly poses.
"Come join the party, leave worries behind!"
I laughed so hard, I felt a bit blind.

A playful rabbit hopped right on cue,
"Don't mind the tangle, it's good for you!"
With every twist, I found something grand,
The tangled knots taught me to stand.

So here I linger, embraced by the wild,
Nature's snare, oh, I've been beguiled.
With giggles and grins in this vibrant land,
I'm a happy captive of nature's hand!

The Dance of Shadows and Sunlight

Beneath the leafy canopies,
A squirrel breaks into a jig,
The sunlight plays a game of tag,
While I just laugh and drink my swig.

The shadows waltz in silly loops,
As bees buzz by with cheeky grins,
The groundhogs join, in mismatched shoes,
While sunlight spins, the day begins.

A rabbit trips upon a root,
He scrambles up, all in a huff,
But giggles pop like springtime shoots,
In this wild dance, we laugh enough.

So come, let's join the leafy fun,
And twirl and spin 'neath sunlit skies,
In every misstep, giggles run,
In this grand ball, we're all the prize.

Secrets of the Wildwood Woven

In the thicket whispers sound,
Where hedgehogs gossip, sly and sly,
And ivy gives a knowing grin,
As rabbits bounce, their tails held high.

A fox struts by with swagger rare,
His fluffy tail a pom-pom show,
They scheme to steal the autumn air,
While mushrooms hide, all in a row.

Oh, the secrets that they share,
Behind the trees and tangled vines,
With every snicker in the air,
Nature's jesters weave their designs.

So if you hear a chuckle low,
Amongst the leaves and rhymes of sun,
Know wildwood's laughter thrives and grows,
With every secret, wrapped in fun.

In the Embrace of Ancient Roots

A tree with arms of gnarled grace,
Invites the critters to come play,
Its roots like fingers, soft to trace,
As squirrels leap, hip-hip hooray!

The raccoons start a midnight feast,
With acorn hats and berry pies,
As owls hoot like they're quite the beast,
In this grand night full of sighs.

What tales the elder roots could tell,
Of silly fights and wild repairs,
In laughter, they weave a cozy spell,
While moonlight peeks and softly stares.

So gather 'round, my woodland friends,
Under the stars, let's share a cheer,
With every giggle, joy transcends,
In roots embraced, we've nothing to fear.

Between Twisted Green and Wild Blue

The vines converge with cheeky flair,
Where butterflies don't feel the heat,
And frogs croak jokes in open air,
While dragonflies perform a feat.

The sky up high, a canvas vast,
For clouds that dance, a ballet bright,
And every breeze just wants to blast,
Through leafy laughter, pure delight.

A picnic planned beneath the boughs,
With sandwiches of leafy green,
But ants declare their own book vows,
As crumbs turn into happy scenes.

So join the fun, let's sway and twirl,
Between the green and blues galore,
In nature's joke, a merry whirl,
Where laughter sprinkles evermore.

The Serpent's Embrace of Flora

A snake in a garden, what a sight,
Wrapping around flowers, oh, what a fright!
Chasing butterflies, but slips and falls,
In a patch of daisies, he trips and calls.

The daisies giggle, they know his name,
His dance is quirky, never the same.
With every twist, he breaks a bloom,
A jungle of laughter thrives in the gloom.

He whispers to roses, full of charm,
"Don't mind my squirm, I'm here to disarm!"
But petals are nervous, oh dear me,
As the wriggly twister climbs up the tree!

In this floral snare, our snake finds glee,
Creating a ruckus, a carefree spree.
With a wink and wiggle, he steals the show,
In the garden of giggles, he's the star, you know!

In the Grip of Leafy Lattice

Underneath the leaves, a party's begun,
A squirrel in a tux, thinks he's so fun.
He dances on branches, a sight quite absurd,
While raccoons applaud, they squeak and they blur.

The vines start to sway, creating a stage,
While blossom-chains cheer, a colorful page.
A chipmunk tap-dances, far, oh so loud,
As the audience gathers, an uproarious crowd.

With acorns for snacks and nectar to sip,
The leafy party grows, oh what a trip!
In a lattice of laughter, they're lost in the cheer,
Who knew leafy vines could bring such good near?

Just a viney embrace, so cozy and tight,
Where flora and fauna unite with delight.
With a shimmy and shake, in nature's grand plot,
They dance through the night; can you believe it or not?

Roots and Reaches: A Green Tapestry

In a world of roots, a cavorting tree,
Whispered secrets and giggles, oh me!
Its limbs play tag with the rays of the sun,
While foxes spin tales of how it's all fun.

Through fingers of ivy, they weave a grand tune,
As squirrels do the can-can with a dandy raccoon.
A dapper old owl hoots from high in his nest,
"Join in, my friends! Let's dance with zest!"

With every twist and turn, the petals all sway,
While laughter takes flight and chases dismay.
Oh, to be rooted where joy knows no bounds,
With each giddy giggle, true happiness sounds.

Just a festival under the canopy wide,
The orchestra's buzzing, with foliage pride.
In laughter and roots, they find their sweet craft,
In this green tapestry, a jolly old draft!

Leaves Covering the Forgotten

Once a grand statue, now just a joke,
Covered in leaves, where the squirrels poke.
"Where's your elegance?" they quip with a grin,
"Oh look at the moss, isn't it a win?"

The once proud knight covered in green,
With relatives old who've never been seen.
He sighs in defeat as he starts to decay,
While frogs croak ballads of his glorious day.

Lost in the flora, he chuckles aloud,
As he joins in the laughter, no need to feel proud.
With vines as his hair and daisies for eyes,
He finds peace in nature, beneath the bright skies.

Now a quirky monument of leaf and cheer,
He waves to the critters that gather near.
With each playful poke, he remembers with ease,
That being a statue can be quite a breeze!

www.ingramcontent.com/pod-product-compliance
Lightning Source LLC
Chambersburg PA
CBHW072121070526
44585CB00016B/1518